Contents

Coral crisis	4
Our blue planet	6
Why oceans matter	8
Warming up	10
Meltdown	12
Carbon crisis	14
Key to ocean life	16
A fishy business	18
Plundering the deep	20
Poisoned seas	22
Disappearing life	24
Seaside alert	26
Protecting our planet	28
Glossary	30
Further information	31
Index	32

Coral crisis

From the deepest black waters to the warmer sunlit waves, oceans and seas are habitats for millions of animals and plants. But human activity, on land and at sea, is endangering some of the world's unique habitats. Some coral reefs began forming 50 million years ago – but careless divers or a dropped anchor can take just seconds to harm them.

▼ *The Great Barrier Reef is threatened by climate change.*

JR PLANET

Destroying the Oceans

Sarah Levete

First published in 2009 by Wayland
Copyright © Wayland 2009

This paperback edition published in 2012 by Wayland.

Wayland, 338 Euston Road, London NW1 3BH
Wayland, Level 17/207 Kent Street, Sydney, NSW 2000

British Library Cataloguing in Publication Data
Levete, Sarah
Destroying the oceans. – (Protecting our planet)
1. Marine ecology – Juvenile literature 2. Marine pollution
– Juvenile literature 3. Marine resources conservation –
Juvenile literature
I. Title
333.9'16416

Produced for Wayland by Calcium
Design: Paul Myerscough
Editor: Sarah Eason
Editor for Wayland: Camilla Lloyd
Illustrations: Geoff Ward
Picture research: Maria Joannou
Consultant: Michael Scott OBE

ISBN 978-0-7502-6841-7

Printed in China

Ardea: Kurt Amsler 5; **Corbis:** Stephen Frink 2b, Kimimasa Mayama/Reuters 5c, Denis Scott 16;
Dreamstime: Donald Blais 11b, Gaja 12–13, Ge Gao 15, Sculpies 21t, Wsroberts 20; **Fotolia:** Freesurf 29; **Istockphoto:**
23, Dave Everitt 27t, Greg Gardner 22, Nancy Nehring 17, Dejan Sarman 25; **Rex Features:** Nature Picture Library 7;
Shutterstock: AioK 13, Annetje 28–29, Ian Bracegirdle 14–15, Lawrence Cruciana 27b, Digitalife 6, EcoPrint 9,
Fouquin 11t, Eric Gevaert 19, 26–27, Daniel Gustavsson 24–25, Irabel8 8–9, Sebastian Kaulitzki 6–7,
David Mckee 18–19, Mollypix 10–11, Darko Novakovic 22–23, Ocean Image Photography 20–21, Dennis Sabo 16–17,
Ian Scott 4–5, Specta 1, 3, 30–31, 32, John Wollwerth 24, Elena Yakusheva 18.

Cover photograph: **Corbis** (Stephen Frink)

Wayland is a division of Hachette Children's Books, an Hachette UK company.

www.hachette.co.uk

CASE STUDY

The Great Barrier Reef

The Great Barrier Reef is the largest natural feature on Earth, stretching more than 2,300 km along the coast of Australia. It can even be seen from space! This vast structure is home to millions of different species of plants and animals. The stony coral is built by lots of coral polyps. These are delicate animals that build protective shells or skeletons around themselves. The coral reef forms from these sea skeletons.

The Great Barrier Reef is a vast network of about 2,900 coral reefs. The colourful reefs swarm with **marine** life. From angelfish to sea fans, coral reefs are home to a quarter of the world's marine animals and plants. The incredible **biodiversity** (range of life) in the reef is under threat.

Pollution, climate change, certain fishing methods and tourism have all contributed to the destruction of this **environment**. Boat loads of tourists flock to visit the colourful reefs, but if a boat carelessly drops anchor on to coral, the fragile shells can smash.

Coral should be colourful, but some is turning white. Many scientists believe that this is due to the effects of **global warming**. Burning **fossil fuels** (see pages 10–11) to provide energy has increased the air temperature globally. A coral's natural **ecosystem** begins to change – and the coral loses its colour.

Human activity has ➤ damaged a quarter of the world's coral reefs.

Our blue planet

The Pacific, Atlantic, Indian, Southern and Arctic oceans cover two-thirds of the Earth's surface. The waters flow from one ocean to another, in a continuous chain around the Earth. The salty oceans and seas (a sea is an area of water within an ocean) are home to millions of animals and plants.

Raining oceans

When Earth formed about 4,000 million years ago, its surface was boiling hot. **Water vapour** filled the air. As the vapour cooled, it turned to liquid water, falling into hollows, called basins, in the Earth's crust. Over millions of years, oceans formed. **Minerals**, such as salt, washed off rocks into the ocean basins, making the water salty.

Fact bank

- 97 per cent of the Earth's water is held in the oceans.

- The Pacific Ocean covers about a third of the Earth, stretching almost halfway round the world.

- The largest mountain range on planet Earth is underwater, deep in the Atlantic Ocean.

◄ Satellite pictures like this one and deep-sea submersibles (underwater craft) have helped us to discover new species and underwater land masses.

6

The anglerfish dwells in the dark, deeper waters. It uses a light above its head to attract fish into its mouth.

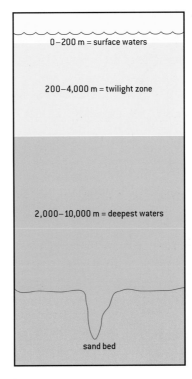

0–200 m = surface waters

200–4,000 m = twilight zone

2,000–10,000 m = deepest waters

sand bed

The oceans are divided into three zones: surface waters; twilight zone; and deepest waters.

Moving oceans

The Earth's crust is made of about 12 **tectonic plates**, fitting together like pieces in a jigsaw. The plates form the ocean floor. Movement and heat deep in the Earth's core keep these jigsaw-like pieces moving very slowly.

Ocean zones

To help understand the ecosystems of the oceans, scientists have divided the depths into three zones. Life exists in each zone and has adapted to the water's conditions – depth of water, temperature and the amount of sunlight it receives. The surface waters of the ocean are warm, heated by the sun's rays. Here, plankton, jellyfish, tuna and herring swim around. Less sunlight reaches the lower twilight zone.

Large-eyed fish such as squid patrol these darker, cooler waters. In the deepest zone it is icy cold and inky dark, and other types of marine life have adapted well to such conditions.

Why oceans matter

A day by the seaside splashing in the waves is fun, but these waves are also crucial for the Earth's survival. The waters of the oceans shape the weather, the land and the world's temperature. Sea creatures provide food for billions of people around the world. Life on land depends on the oceans.

Water on the move

The oceans are part of a system that influences the climate from Europe to Australia. Seawater moves around the world constantly, in massive bands of water called **currents**. This movement is like a non-stop conveyor belt – it takes about 1,000 years for the belt to make one complete trip around the world. Ocean currents flow in complex patterns, driven by the wind and the heat of the water (heat which has been absorbed from the sun's rays). Some currents are also driven by the salinity of the water (how salty it is) – cold, salty water is denser (heavier) than warm water so it sinks. Warm ocean currents heat the air above them. When the air moves over land, it warms the local climate. Cold water currents cool the air and the local climate.

Warm and cold water currents flow around the Earth's oceans and seas. They also affect the climate around the world. ➤

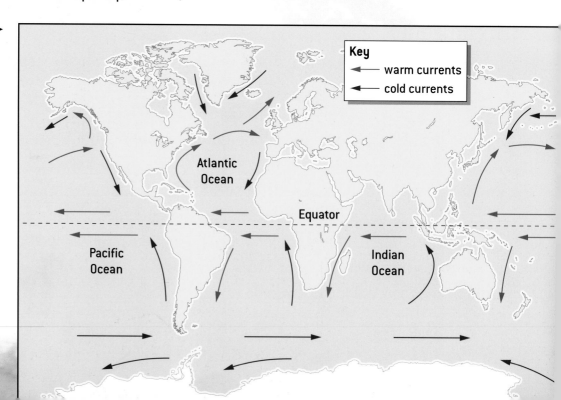

Key
- ← warm currents
- ← cold currents

Atlantic Ocean

Equator

Pacific Ocean

Indian Ocean

Goodness from waste

Waste such as dead organisms sink to the ocean floor, if they are not gobbled up by other creatures on the way down. Organisms called **bacteria** break down the remains into **nutrients**. In a process called **upwelling**, rising waters carry these nutrients back to the surface waters.

Ocean life

Millions of years ago, life began in the oceans as tiny organisms. Today, the oceans' biodiversity is found in habitats such as coral reefs, mangrove forests, and seagrass meadows. These habitats also protect the coastline from **erosion** (wearing away) and flooding.

CASE STUDY

The Gulf Stream

The Gulf Stream is an ocean current. It carries warm tropical water from the Caribbean Sea and the Gulf of Mexico across the North Atlantic to Europe. The warm water heats the air above it, and the movement of this warm air carries heat towards the north. Without the Gulf Stream, northern Europe would be much colder.

"The oceans exert a profound [deep] influence on mankind and indeed upon all forms of life on Earth."

Roger Revell, a founder of the Intergovernmental Oceanographic Commission of UNESCO

▼ *All over the world, people depend on the oceans' fish supplies as a source of food.*

Warming up

The climate has always changed, but climate change is the term used to describe the current global weather chaos. What is happening to the weather, and who is to blame? And what has it got to do with the sea?

Burning fuels, heating up

The gas carbon dioxide (CO_2) is the major contributor to global warming, or the worldwide increase in temperature. Most of the energy we use, from petrol for cars to electricity for a computer, comes from burning fossil fuels in power stations. These fossil fuels include coal, oil and gas. When burned, oil and coal release large amounts of carbon dioxide.

"Climate change is a reality – one of the most serious threats facing humanity today."

Richard Kinley, United Nations, 2005

◄ *Powerful, crashing waves are a beautiful sight. But we also need to be aware of the oceans' dangers, such as tsunamis.*

The right amount of carbon dioxide in the atmosphere naturally keeps the Earth's temperature in balance. Too much carbon dioxide traps in excess heat, like a greenhouse. The effect of too much carbon dioxide, known as a greenhouse gas, causes global warming. Since the beginning of the 20th century, the average surface temperature of the Earth has risen by 0.74°C. Scientists predict that a rise in the temperature of more than 2°C risks catastrophe and chaos for life on Earth.

Extreme weather, ➤ such as tsunamis and hurricanes, are becoming more common.

Warmer seas

As the atmosphere warms up, so do the seas. Warmer waters contain less oxygen. Marine animals have to swim to cooler, more oxygen-rich areas, or they can risk suffocating to death. This can affect the **food web** of which many plants and animals are part. Fish, such as tuna and cod, die from too little oxygen. Animals higher up the chain, that feed on the fish, are affected, too.

Extreme weather

Scientists believe that the increase in the number of strong storms is partly due to climate change. Lashing waves can destroy entire villages and reshape coastal areas dramatically. Hurricanes damage land, destroying drains and sewers. Pollution and raw sewage may run freely into the seas.

WHAT CAN BE DONE?

Planet Earth has experienced cycles of climate change before. There was the Ice Age thousands of years ago, as the Earth moved away from the sun. But most scientists agree that today's climate change is rapid and extreme. It is caused by human activity. Adapting our lifestyles can make a difference. Saving energy and using fuels that do not release large quantities of carbon dioxide into the atmosphere can prevent further harm to the planet.

◄ Gulls are fish predators. They can starve if feeding grounds have fewer fish.

Meltdown

The Arctic and Antarctic conjure up images of shiny, white mountains of ice. But could **glaciers** soon be things of the past? These huge, slow-moving blocks of ice built up over thousands of years, and **icebergs** are melting fast because of global warming.

Rising seas

Warmer seas are making sea levels rise. There is much debate about how much more they will rise and how quickly. Even a rise of just one metre by the end of the 21st century could submerge entire countries. That would destroy homes, lives and livelihoods.

Warm water takes up more space than cool water, so it increases the risk of flooding in coastal areas. Low-lying countries such as Bangladesh and the Netherlands are particularly at risk. Unlike the Netherlands, Bangladesh and other developing countries cannot afford sophisticated sea defences to protect them from the rising seas.

▼ *Global warming means that icebergs are melting faster than ever before — especially in the Antarctic.*

CASE STUDY

Polar bears

The majestic, white polar bear patrols the icy Arctic, hunting for seals. Seals swim faster than bears, so the bear lies in wait for seals and their pups to emerge from holes in the sea ice. During the summer and autumn when the ice melts, the bear survives on energy stored in its body from eating seals caught in the icy months. But warmer weather means longer ice-free periods; this means longer periods without food for the bear. The bears lose weight and this affects their ability to reproduce. Polar bear populations are now in decline.

The United States' government is so concerned about the speed at which the Arctic is melting and the effect on the polar bear, that it has listed the polar bear an endangered species. But some argue that this does not address the cause of the problem. They believe that real changes are needed to protect such animals. Only by large reductions in the amount of carbon dioxide and other greenhouse gases released into the atmosphere can we stop the effect of global warming and halt the rapid melting of the polar bear's **habitat**.

▼ *Polar bears need sea ice to survive. From these ice platforms they can hunt seals and other wildlife.*

Carbon crisis

Carbon is a key substance in all living organisms. Carbon passes through different cycles in different ecosystems. These cycles, such as the action of trees in soaking up carbon dioxide and releasing oxygen, maintain a healthy balance of carbon dioxide in the air and on land.

Natural balance

The vast, swirling oceans absorb carbon dioxide in the air. The gas dissolves into the ocean and is carried to the ocean bed by sinking currents. Hundreds of years later this water rises to the surface again, where it warms. The carbon dioxide carried by the water is then re-absorbed into the atmosphere. In this way, the oceans help to keep the amount of carbon dioxide gas in air in an even balance.

◄ *Generating electricity by burning fossil fuels creates a lot of carbon dioxide. About a third of the gas in air dissolves into the cold oceans.*

Disrupting the balance

Human activity over the last 200 years has released massive amounts of carbon dioxide into the atmosphere. This is mainly from burning fossil fuels such as oil and coal. If there is too much carbon dioxide in the atmosphere, there is also too much carbon dioxide in the deep oceans. This can threaten life in the oceans.

Fragile shells

Too much carbon in the oceans changes the **chemistry** of the seas. The seawater becomes too **acidic**. This reduces the strength of a mineral called calcium carbonate, which many sea creatures use to grow shells.

◄ *Tiny, shelled pteropod species are affected by acidic waters.*

▲ *Vast areas of forest in China have been cut down to make way for farmland and new towns. The tracks in the hills are for logging lorries.*

Rising levels of carbon dioxide threaten the ocean's biodiversity. For instance, the thin shell of marine snails is easily eaten away by acid waters. Salmon, mackerel, herring and cod eat the snails. If there are no snails to eat, the fish go hungry – and their own survival is threatened.

> "Ocean chemistry is changing to a state that has not occurred for hundreds of thousands of years . . . Shell-building by marine organisms will slow down or stop. Reef-building will decrease or reverse."
>
> **Richard Feely, Seattle's Pacific Marine Environmental Laboratory**

WHAT CAN BE DONE?

An excess of carbon dioxide in the atmosphere is damaging marine life and ecosystems. The amount of carbon dioxide gas in the air can be reduced by burning smaller amounts of fossil fuels. Instead of chopping down forests to clear land, we can plant more trees to help absorb excess carbon dioxide. We can use alternative energy sources such as wind and solar power which do not produce large amounts of carbon dioxide.

Key to ocean life

Tiny microscopic plants called phytoplankton help keep the correct balance of carbon dioxide and oxygen in the air. They soak up carbon dioxide in the oceans. If there were fewer sea plants, there would be more carbon dioxide in the atmosphere.

Food chain

The microscopic phytoplankton are crucial to the ocean **food chain**. Without them, the massive blue whale will not have enough to eat! These little plants are eaten by larger zooplankton. Zooplankton are eaten by larger fish who are then gobbled up by the largest creature of all — the blue whale.

Fact bank

- One teaspoon of seawater can contain as many as a million one-celled phytoplankton.

- The world's phytoplankton produce at least half of the oxygen we breathe.

▲ *The blue whale is the top predator of a marine food chain. Food chains link together into food webs.*

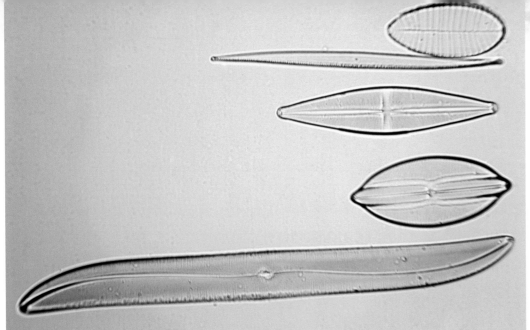

◄ *Phytoplankton form the base of the marine food chain. They support most life in the oceans.*

Answer in the oceans?

Phytoplankton soak up carbon in the oceans. When dead phytoplankton sink to the ocean floor, the carbon settles there, then is covered by other sinking dead matter. In this way, the oceans act as a sink, somewhere to get rid of carbon, which would otherwise build up in the atmosphere.

Would it be possible to make the ocean soak up even more carbon dioxide from the atmosphere by creating even more phytoplankton? Some scientists believe that adding quantities of iron to the ocean waters increases the population of phytoplankton. They argue that this increases the amount of carbon dioxide they soak up. This is called ocean

fertilisation. There is much debate as to the benefits of ocean fertilisation. As we have seen, too much carbon dioxide can interfere with the levels of oxygen in the seas – killing off many species.

> *"Without phytoplankton, life on earth as we know it would never have happened and without them, it would cease to exist."*
>
> **Gene Carl Feldman, NASA oceanographer**

▼ *All ocean life, from coral reefs to giant whales, could be threatened if the amount of carbon dioxide in the water becomes too high.*

A fishy business

Millions of people depend upon fishing for their livelihoods and for fish as their main source of protein. But some methods of fishing are destroying entire species, and even threatening the ocean's biodiversity.

Changes in fishing

Some communities continue to fish using traditional methods, such as rods and lines, spears and hand-made traps. These skills and methods are passed down from generation to generation. Generally, these methods do not alter the balance of life in the deep. However, large-scale fishing industries have created great changes deep underwater.

▲ *Traditional methods of fishing cause much less damage to the environment.*

If we do not stop ➤ *overfishing the Earth's oceans, some species of fish may disappear for good.*

Fleets of ships lower massive trawler nets that scoop up any creature from the ocean floor, even those that are not being fished. Dolphins and turtles get caught in the nets. Longline boats trail massive lines of hooks set with bait to catch tuna or swordfish. The bait also attracts seabirds, such as albatrosses. As the birds bite, the hooks drag them under the water – and the birds drown.

Trashing the sea floor

Some boats use bottom trawling to catch deep-sea fish. Massive nets, sometimes weighed down with rubber tyres, drag along the ocean floor. The net destroys everything in its path such as deep-sea corals and sponges. These animals grow just a few millimetres each year and live for thousands of years. One trawl can destroy centuries of growth.

WHAT CAN BE DONE?

Some species of fish, such as cod and orange roughy, cannot reproduce as quickly as they are caught. When too many fish are caught too quickly, this is called **overfishing**. It can threaten entire species of fish. How can we fish in a **sustainable** way, without fishing out of existence the very animals we eat? Fish farming may be a way to create a more sustainable supply of fish. For example, fish such as salmon can be bred in areas called fish farms. This does not use up the stocks of salmon in the seas.

Large-scale fishing industries can deplete the oceans' stocks of fish and wildlife.

Plundering the deep

As we discover more about the ocean floor, the more we see the riches it offers us — from oil to gas. But diving deep for these unique resources can harm the oceans' delicate ecosystems.

Stores of oil

We need oil and gas to run our cars, homes and industries. More than one-fifth of the world's oil and gas supplies are **plundered** from under the sea bed. When plankton die,

CASE STUDY

Marine medicine

From sea sponges to horseshoe crabs, scientists are investigating sea creatures that can help human health. Substances in a range of marine creatures can form the base for new drugs that can help improve our health.

Some deep-sea sponges produce substances that could be used to treat diseases such as cancers. Certain substances in the horseshoe crab's blood protect it from harmful bacteria.

Blood taken from horseshoe crabs is used to check that some medicines do not contain harmful bacteria. NASA (the United States' space organisation) has used substances from this ancient crab to help detect any unwelcome germs or bacteria in its spacecraft.

The horseshoe crab is a very useful ➤
creature in scientific research.

they sink to the bottom of the sea, buried by sand and mud. Plankton that died millions of years ago form the source of today's oil and gas from the ocean. The pressure and temperature underground turn substances from the decaying animals and plants into oil and gas. Oil and gas slowly move up through rocks.

Finding and drilling for reserves of oil and gas deep in the sea is a complex, expensive operation. It also plays havoc with the ocean's ecosystem. Currently the United States' government is thinking about whether to allow drilling for oil and gas in the Arctic Ocean. This could destroy the polar bear's habitat, already under threat from global warming.

▲ *Oil rigs are a familiar sight on the surface of our seas and oceans. But they can cause great damage to the ocean floor.*

methane. The methane hydrates could become an important future fuel source. However, like carbon dioxide, methane is a greenhouse gas. Scientists do not know the effect of releasing the gas on global warming.

Frozen gas

Methane is a major part of natural gas, a useful fuel. Scientists have discovered stores of ice, called methane hydrates, a few metres beneath the sea bed. This ice contains

The oceans' ➤ *colourful coral gardens are under threat from damage caused by human activity.*

21

Poisoned seas

We swim, dive and ride the ocean waves. We eat food from the seas. But these masses of beautiful, swirling blue waters are often full of chemicals and poisons. Are we destroying the very waters that we rely upon so much?

Monster growth of plants

Farmers use chemicals in fertilisers on their land to help crops grow. The chemicals seep into the ground and eventually run back into rivers and then seas. These fertilisers make tiny sea plants such as algae grow more quickly in the seas. Bacteria eat the algae, using up much of the ocean's oxygen supplies. Without oxygen, it is difficult for other marine creatures to survive. Areas in the seas without oxygen are called dead zones. The number of dead zones is increasing.

◄ *Spraying crops with pesticides adds chemicals to the land, rivers and seas. The chemicals can harm marine animals.*

Swimming with human waste

Sewage or human waste flows into the seas you swim in. If the sewage has not been treated and cleaned, it carries bacteria that spread diseases. Strong storms and heavy rains flood land. Drains can collapse and then sewage flows into the blue seas. Cruise ships cross the seas, dumping untreated sewage into the clear waters. Each day, a standard cruise ship produces 114,000 litres of sewage from toilets and 852,000 litres of sewage from the sinks and showers.

▲ *Plastic waste can be particularly dangerous to sea creatures by suffocating them.*

Plastic bags kill

After a picnic on the beach, a discarded plastic bag blows into the sea. Carried away on the waves, it floats out to the deeper seas. Here, a deep-sea turtle tries to swallow the bag, thinking it is a jellyfish to eat. The sea turtle suffocates. More than a million seabirds and 100,000 mammals and sea turtles die each year by getting tangled in or by eating plastics.

WHAT CAN BE DONE?

When an oil tanker runs aground or crashes, the disaster makes headline news. The oil slick can spread for thousands of kilometres, coating any wildlife in the sticky slime. But such disasters make up only 5 per cent of the oil pollution in the seas. Some comes from everyday leaks from tankers. Even more comes from oil, such as oil used in car engines, that ends up being flushed down drains. Recycle oil instead of letting it disappear down a drain where it ends up back in the sea, causing harm. There are many oil recycling centres around the country.

▼ *Areas of the Earth's oceans that once teemed with life can become dead zones when pollutants such as oil and other chemicals spill into them.*

Disappearing life

From chopping down forests to leaking chemicals into the water, human activity is meddling with the natural balance of ocean life. This can have serious consequences for the ocean's biodiversity, and even human safety on land.

Alien invasion

Before loading cargo and sailing, ships fill up tanks with seawater called ballast water. This helps the ship to maintain stability and to change position in the water. Animals and plants are often in the ballast water. When ships dock and unload the cargo, they release the ballast water back into the oceans, along with any surviving plants and animals caught up in the water.

By docking in another country's waters, ships may introduce alien life. A North American creature like a jellyfish called a comb jelly arrived in ballast water in the Black Sea. It gobbled up most of the phytoplankton and zooplankton and native fish eggs. Local fish species were wiped out. The comb jelly continues to wreak havoc with ecosystems across the world, as it travels as an unwanted guest in ballast water.

> "Over the past few centuries, invasive alien species have caused untold damage to natural ecosystems and human economies alike."
>
> **Klaus Toepfer, Executive Director of the United Nations Environment Programme**

Some scientists believe that the comb ➤ jelly is one of the earliest creatures to have ever lived on the planet.

Disappearing dugongs

Dugongs are large grey mammals, sometimes called sea cows because of the large amounts of seagrass they eat. However, dugong populations are threatened with the loss of their feeding grounds – meadows of seagrass. These are destroyed by mining, pollution or the effect of fishing. Dugongs that are swimming in coastal waters are also killed by speeding boats.

▲ *Dugongs use huge, paddle-like forelimbs to move around as they search for food.*

CASE STUDY

Natural protection

In tropical climates such as South-east Asia, mangrove forests fringe the area between rainforests and seas. The tangled, snaking roots of mangrove trees (see below) trap sediment from flowing rivers. This helps to slow down the flow of water and protects the land from erosion, often caused by fierce waves and winds.

Mangrove forests are one of the world's most threatened habitats.

Cut down to use the trees as timber or to provide land for fish farming, the forests are disappearing fast. This destroys the natural barrier on land against fierce storms and raging waves. The violent tsunami (massive wave) of 2004 that swept over coastal areas in southern Asia killed thousands and swallowed up entire villages. Just two people died in one village that was surrounded by thick mangrove forests; 6,000 people died in a nearby village which did not have similar forest cover.

◄ *People are cutting down mangrove forests along parts of Asia's coastline. Many fish and animals live among the mangrove roots – if the forests disappear, these creatures will, too.*

Seaside alert

When the sun shines, tourists flock to sandy beaches, and oceans become littered. Coastal towns across the world are built up with hotels, restaurants and holiday resorts. But building up these resorts has a significant environmental impact. Habitats are destroyed.

Wearing away the coast

Wearing away of the land, erosion, is a natural process, but human activity is making the problem worse. Around the world, waves are slowly swallowing up coastlines as buildings take the place of sand dunes. Rising sea levels caused by global warming make waves crash further inland. Dams are built across rivers to divert them for freshwater supplies. This stops the flow of gravel and other small pieces of material called **sediment** from reaching the coastline. This makes the coastline more likely to wash away with the waves. Planting trees instead of hotels can help to prevent the speed of the coast's erosion.

▲ *Grassy sand dunes provide a natural barrier to erosion by the waves.*

This is The Palm in Dubai which is a huge residential and tourist project.

Artificial islands

Engineers are currently building luxury islands off the coast of Dubai. They will house hotels, restaurants, sports clubs and homes. Building any large and artificial structure in the sea disrupts the natural **ecology**. No one yet knows the long-term effect on the oceans' ecosystems of building such structures.

CASE STUDY

Loggerhead turtles

Boa Vista is an island in West Africa. Part of the Cape Verde group of islands, it is a nesting place for thousands of loggerhead turtles. From May to September, the turtles crawl from the sea to find a safe place in the sand to lay their eggs.

Hardly any turtles remain on Cape Verde's other islands. Their nesting grounds have been taken over by tourists enjoying the long sandy beaches. Now, there are plans to build an airport at Boa Vista, to encourage more tourists to visit. New hotels are planned. Many local people want to attract more tourists as this helps provide work for population. Others

believe that this could seriously disturb the nesting ground for loggerhead turtles.

Ecotourism

Tourism can have a negative effect on the ocean and coastline. But there is a more environmentally friendly way of enjoying our planet. Ecotourism means respecting the environment so that it continues to provide a haven for both humans and animals for years to come.

Loggerhead turtles like to lay their eggs on many ► of the sandy beaches enjoyed by tourists.

Protecting our planet

We cannot undo the effect of human activities so far. But we can work towards sustainable solutions to the problems. These can minimise negative effects and put in place a better environment for future generations.

No fishing allowed

In 'No Take Zones' in the oceans you cannot catch certain fish in a certain area. This allows fish to slowly return to their natural populations. This also benefits the surrounding seas as the increasing numbers of fish from the 'No Take Zones' spread into other areas. Marine reserves are like national parks in the sea. They are areas where ocean habitats and creatures are protected.

"Humans will always use the oceans for recreation, extraction of resources, and for commercial activity such as shipping. This is a good thing. Our goal, and really our necessity, is to do this in a sustainable way so that our oceans remain in a healthy state and continue to provide us with the resources we need and want.

Ben Halpern, research scientist at the University of California, Santa Barbara, United States

◄ *The oceans support a staggering variety of life. We need to look after our oceans.*

Laws

Governments can lay down laws to protect the oceans. For instance, countries in the European Union now have to "take the necessary action to achieve or maintain good environmental status in the marine environment by 2020". The goal is to work towards seas that are "clean, safe, healthy, biologically diverse and productive".

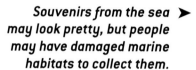

Souvenirs from the sea ➤ may look pretty, but people may have damaged marine habitats to collect them.

HOW CAN WE PROTECT OUR PLANET?

There are things that we can all do to help protect our seas and oceans.

- Does the fish you eat come from a sustainable source? Check any packaging.

- Whenever you take a trip to the seaside, always take your litter home with you. Remember that a plastic bag can kill a dolphin.

- Think about where things come from. A colourful piece of coral in the shop may have come from a living coral reef, which becomes damaged as it is plundered.

- Be energy-wise. The energy that we use from burning fossil fuels such as oil, gas and coal increases global warming. This has a direct effect on the seas and oceans of the world.

- Encourage your school or local authority to investigate the possibilities of using energy from solar power or other 'green' energy sources. Alternatives to fossil fuels can benefit everyone.

- Enjoy the oceans and their incredible richness. Protect them for the future.

Glossary

acidic when a liquid contains more acid than alkali, which may be harmful

bacteria tiny organisms

biodiversity range of life

chemistry the structure or make-up of a substance, such as water

currents bands of water driven by winds

ecology the relationship between living things and their environment

ecosystem balance between a community of animals and plants and its environment

environment the surroundings

erosion wearing away

food chain the way that animals and plants are linked by what eats what

food web the linked feeding relationships between different species

fossil fuels fuels such as oil, coal and gas. These fuels formed from the remains of plants and animals

glaciers massive blocks of snow that freeze into ice, built up over thousands of years

global warming the gradual warming of Earth's climate

icebergs edges of a glacier that have broken off into the ocean

habitat home

marine to do with the oceans and seas

minerals hard substances found in the ground

nutrients goodness from food needed for life

overfishing catching too many fish before they can naturally reproduce and replenish stocks

tectonic plates giant slabs of the Earth's crust

plundered robbed

sediment small bits of sand and soil that wash away from the land in rivers

sustainable managing resources in a way that protects the environment and the resource

upwelling the movement of nutrients from the deep sea to the surface

water vapour the form of water as a gas in the air

Further information

Books

Water (Energy Files) by Steve Parker (Heinemann, 2003)

Protecting Habitats (Action for the Environment) by R. Bellamy
(Franklin Watts, 2006)

Seas and Oceans (Caring for the Planet) by Neil Champion
(Franklin Watts, 2006)

Environments (Sustainable World) by Rob Bowden (Wayland, 2007)

Oceans in Danger (Protecting Habitats) by Anita Ganeri
(Franklin Watts, 2008)

Websites

Find out more about the threats to our oceans at the Greenpeace
website:
www.greenpeace.org.uk

This website has useful links to other sites about the world's oceans:
www.seafriends.org.nz/oceano

Index

alternative energy 15, 29
Antarctic 12
Arctic 12, 13

Bangladesh 12
blue whale 16

carbon dioxide 10, 11, 13, 14–15, 16, 17, 21
climate change 4, 5, 8, 10, 11
coastal erosion 9, 11, 25, 26
comb jelly 24
coral 4–5, 9, 17, 19, 21, 29

dead zones 22, 23
dugongs 25

fertilisers 22
fishing 5, 9, 18–19, 25, 28
flooding 9, 12, 23
food chain 16
fossil fuels 5, 10, 14, 15, 29

glaciers 12
global warming 5, 10, 11, 12, 13, 21, 26, 29
Great Barrier Reef, Australia 4, 5
greenhouse gases 11, 13, 21
Gulf Stream 9

horseshoe crab 20

icebergs 12

loggerhead turtles 27

mangrove forests 9, 25
marine reserves 28
medicine 20
methane 21

Netherlands 12

ocean currents 8, 9, 14
ocean fertilisation 17
ocean zones 7
oxygen 11, 14, 16, 17, 22

pesticides 22
phytoplankton 16, 17, 24
plastic bags 23, 29
pollution 5, 11, 23, 25

sand dunes 26
sea levels 12, 26
seagrass 9, 25
sewage 11, 23
storms 11, 23, 25

tectonic plates 7
tourism 5, 26, 27

zooplankton 16, 24

PLAY THE PART

SHOPKEEPER

Written by Liz Gogerly

Photographs by Chris Fairclough

WAYLAND

First published in paperback in 2015
by Wayland

Copyright © Wayland 2015

Wayland
An imprint of
Hachette Children's Group
Part of Hodder & Stoughton
Carmelite House
50 Victoria Embankment
London EC4Y 0DZ

Editors: Paul Humphrey, James Nixon
Design: D. R. ink
Commissioned photography: Chris Fairclough
Model maker: Tom Humphrey

Picture credits: J Sainsbury plc: p. 12 left; Shutterstock: pp. 5 bottom (Kzenon),
7 top (Stephen Coburn), 8 top (Dimitriy Shironosov).

Dewey Number: 381.1-dc22
ISBN: 978 0 7502 9706 6
Library ebook ISBN: 978 0 7502 7265 0

10 9 8 7 6 5 4 3 2 1

Printed in China

An Hachette UK Company
www.hachette.co.uk
www.hachettechildrens.co.uk

The author, packager and publisher would like
to thank Davigdor Infants' School, Hove for
their help and participation in this book.